Writing from Research

for Christian Schools®

Grace Collins Hargis

Bob Jones University Press, Greenville, SC 29614

This textbook was written by members of the faculty and staff of Bob Jones University. Standing for the "old-time religion" and the absolute authority of the Bible since 1927, Bob Jones University is the world's leading Fundamentalist Christian university. The staff of the University is devoted to educating Christian men and women to be servants of Jesus Christ in all walks of life.

Providing unparalleled academic excellence, Bob Jones University prepares its students through its offering of over one hundred majors, while its fervent spiritual emphasis prepares their minds and hearts for service and devotion to the Lord Jesus Christ.

If you would like more information about the spiritual and academic opportunities available at Bob Jones University, please call
1-800-BJ-AND-ME (1-800-252-6363).

Cover photographs by Corel Corporation.

NOTE:
The fact that materials produced by other publishers are referred to in this volume does not constitute an endorsement by Bob Jones University Press of the content or theological position of materials produced by such publishers. The position of Bob Jones University Press, and of the University itself, is well known. Any references and ancillary materials are listed as an aid to the student or the teacher and in an attempt to maintain the accepted academic standards of the publishing industry.

WRITING FROM RESEARCH for Christian Schools®

Grace Collins Hargis, Ph.D.

for Christian Schools is a registered trademark of Bob Jones University Press.

© 1998 Bob Jones University Press
Greenville, South Carolina 29614

ISBN 1-57924-075-5

15 14 13 12 11 10 9 8 7 6 5 4

TABLE OF CONTENTS

To the Teacher

Writing from Research supports different subject areas in which research writing projects may be useful. Chapter 1 surveys the whole process of researching and writing, and then Chapter 2 presents the widely used MLA style for documenting sources.

Chapters 3 and 4 deal with writing from research in the sciences. Chapter 3 explains the usual organization of scientific papers, and Chapter 4 demonstrates how to acknowledge sources in the sciences. These chapters are useful not only for those teaching science and their students but also for students (and their parental advisors) who are preparing science fair projects and papers.

The Teacher's Edition contains an Appendix that provides junior high and high school English teachers with ideas for optional research projects. Although a major research project is probably best reserved for upper high school, other students can benefit from an interesting introduction to the research process.

Thus English teachers and students find their needs met through Chapters 1, 2, and the Appendix. Those in history and other nonscience courses will profit from the first two chapters. Science teachers and students can use Chapters 1, 3, and 4. Science fair contestants (beginning perhaps as early as grade 7) can focus on Chapters 3 and 4. Teachers in all disciplines will find helpful teaching notes in the Teacher's Edition.

Many student writers now have access to personal computers. In the overview chapter (Chapter 1), these students will find suggestions for using computers in the research and writing phases. The two chapters on documentation styles include ways to acknowledge electronic sources, both online sources and portable media such as compact disks.

CHAPTER 1

Research Writing: The Whole Process

Have you ever tried to reach an unfamiliar destination with inaccurate or incomplete directions and no map? Even if you reached your intended location, the trip was probably an exasperating experience. The same holds true when writing a research paper: if your directions are not thorough, the journey from brainstorming to the final paper will be a frustrating one. This book is designed to help you write a successful research paper through accurate instructions and a detailed map—the flow chart below.

The flow chart shows you the entire process of researching and writing the paper. It may look complicated, but only because it is broken down into individual steps. If you follow the main path down the middle, you will go through all the steps. The side comments give you suggestions to help you with four of the steps.

Read through the flow chart now. You can use it by itself, or it can be a reference and an overview for the following discussion.

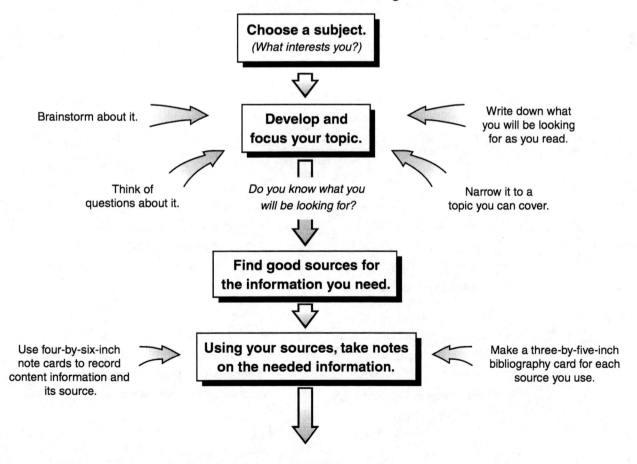

Choose a subject.
(What interests you?)

Brainstorm about it. → Develop and focus your topic. ← Write down what you will be looking for as you read.

Think of questions about it. → *Do you know what you will be looking for?* ← Narrow it to a topic you can cover.

Find good sources for the information you need.

Use four-by-six-inch note cards to record content information and its source. → Using your sources, take notes on the needed information. ← Make a three-by-five-inch bibliography card for each source you use.

Organize your note cards and write an outline for the paper. Write your thesis (the main idea).

Do you have enough information? Is the paper's direction clear to you?

Present your own thinking as well as what you have learned.

As you write, record the source and page numbers from each note card you use.

Write the first draft in one sitting, if possible.

Write the facts in your own words whenever you can.

Use quotation marks for any quoted phrase or sentence.

Let the paper rest for a day or two.

Read and rethink your paper. Revise and edit as needed.

Prepare the title page.

Complete the paper.

Prepare the source list.

Prepare the final outline, if needed.

Are you using a computer or a word processor?

Finalize the source citations in the text.

Yes **No**

Print out a semifinal copy and proofread it carefully.

Type your final copy.

Make corrections and print the final copy.

Proofread it carefully and make minor corrections neatly. If needed, retype a page.

Choose a Subject

If your subject is not assigned, try to come up with a topic that really interests you. You will enjoy your research more, and the knowledge you gain may turn out to be more helpful to you personally. (If your subject *is* assigned, move on to "Focus Your Topic.")

Consider what your interests are and write down some ideas. What do you tend to think about? What do you like to read about or to draw? What makes you curious? What subjects are most interesting to you in school? What area might you like to work with after you finish school?

You might also get some ideas from teachers or from your family. Your parents, for example, may have noticed an area that always seems to catch your attention.

If nothing else seems to work, try writing down an alphabetical list of nouns or noun phrases (Africa, beach erosion, colds, dump trucks, exit ramps, etc.) or verbs and objects (asking questions, buying military supplies, catching fish, doing homework, etc.). Then see what phrases stand out and think about how they could be developed. For example, who invented the dump truck and when? How do dump trucks work? Are there different types of dump trucks? How about other kinds of construction equipment?

Focus Your Topic

First, broaden your view by brainstorming about your subject. To brainstorm by yourself, write down as many ideas as possible that are related to your subject. While you are doing so, do not judge your ideas or cross out any—just keep thinking of more. To keep the ideas flowing, reread your list and get more ideas from what you have written. Afterward, underline or circle the ideas that seem most promising.

Here is an example of brainstorming on the subject of exit ramps.

Exit Ramps
- *important for safety (allow slowing down)*
- *turn lane needed before exit ramp*
- *length of ramp and turn lane—how decided?*
- *entrance ramps the same length etc. as exit ramps?*
- *merge lane needed with entrance ramp*
- *how to merge smoothly, safely*

- *interstate highways—how old an idea? whose? when developed? (history)*
- *any similar highways before interstates were built?*
- *problems of interstate highways (maybe boredom or overcrowding)—solutions*

After writing down these ideas, this person considered them and underlined the ones he liked best. He realized that his interest had broadened to the subject of interstate highways, either their history or their problems. At this point he decided that some exploratory reading would help him see which area would work best.

If you begin without enough information to brainstorm, you can start with exploratory reading in encyclopedia articles or in other sources for nonexperts. Another technique is to think of questions about your subject, as in the earlier example of dump trucks and construction equipment. You and a classmate might try to help one another think of additional questions about your subjects.

Once you have some ideas and a better grasp of the subject area, you can narrow your subject down to a topic that is about the right size for you to handle. For example, instead of construction machinery in general, you might decide to write about site-preparation machinery such as bulldozers or dump trucks.

Now that your topic is focused, make sure you know what to look for as you read. If you can write a tentative outline of your paper, the subtopics on your outline will guide your research. If not, write a list of questions to investigate.

Find Good Sources

If you know what information to look for, you are ready to find good sources, read, and take notes. For the sake of efficiency, you will probably find most of your sources first and then read from them for information. Keep in mind, though, that during the reading phase you may find references to additional good sources. (And as you learn more about your subject, you might discover more areas to investigate.)

If you have not already done some general background reading about your topic in an encyclopedia, do so now. Then go to the library catalog to do a subject search for books and perhaps other works on your topic. If you are not familiar with how to find information in the library, get help from a librarian or your teacher.

As you look for books, be aware of your library's system of classification. Understanding it will help you to find books and to recognize their general contents from their call numbers. For your convenience, both common systems of classification are summarized here.

The Dewey decimal system has ten major headings.

The Dewey Decimal System

000	General works
100	Philosophy and psychology
200	Religion
300	Social sciences
400	Languages
500	Natural sciences and mathematics
600	Applied sciences and technology
700	Fine arts
800	Literature
900	History and geography

For example, a particular book about Stephen Crane, an American author, has the call number 813 / C85c / 1980. The Dewey decimal number is *813,* for American literature. The author number is *C85,* for Stephen Crane; and the small *c* at the end is the initial of the last name of Edwin Cady, the author of this book. The *1980* identifies it as the 1980 revised edition.

The Library of Congress system has twenty-one major headings.

The Library of Congress System

A	General works	**L**	Education
B	Philosophy, psychology, and religion	**M**	Music
		N	Fine arts
C	General history	**P**	Language and literature
D	World history	**Q**	Science
E	American history	**R**	Medicine
F	Local American history	**S**	Agriculture and forestry
G	Geography and anthropology	**T**	Technology and engineering
H	Social sciences	**U**	Military science
J	Political science	**V**	Naval science
K	Law	**Z**	Bibliography and library science

The same book about Stephen Crane in another library has the Library of Congress number PS1449.C85Z575. The first letter is *P* for language and literature, and the subject area is further specified by *S1449*. As in the Dewey decimal system, *C85* identifies Stephen Crane.

As you look for information, broaden your sights beyond books alone. Remember periodicals such as magazines and newspapers; electronic resources, especially online databases and CD-ROM databases; and experts you can interview.

For periodicals, a number of indexes exist. *Readers' Guide to Periodical Literature* will help you find articles in magazines. For news stories and feature articles in major American newspapers, look in the *New York Times Index* and *National Newspaper Index*. There are also specialized indexes in many subject areas, including *General Science Index, Humanities Index,* and *Education Index;* check to see what is available in your subject area.

Some of these indexes may be available to you in book form, and some may be available electronically for a computer search. Searching a CD-ROM or online bibliographic database gives you access to much more information than you could find in a single volume of an annual index or bibliography.

Whether you are searching an electronic database for actual subject information or for references to sources, you can type in the words *or, and,* and *not* to expand or limit your search appropriately. (These words are called *Boolean operators,* named after mathematician George Boole.) *Or* broadens your search because it gives you information with either of two search terms in it. For example, you could search for "Mark Twain *or* Samuel Clemens" in order to get information from sources that use either Clemens's actual name or his pen name, Mark Twain.

And and *not* narrow your search. *And* means that each article or title must have both search terms in it, and *not* means it cannot have the term specified. For example, "pain relievers *not* aspirin" would eliminate unwanted references to aspirin and help you find out about other pain relievers. In order to get comparisons of acetaminophen and ibuprofen, you could search for "acetaminophen *and* ibuprofen"; each record found will refer to both. You can even group your search terms and operators by using parentheses: for example, "pain relievers not (opiates or aspirin)" would eliminate both opiates, such as morphine, and aspirin.

Before you finish your search for information, consider whether you might be able to interview an expert or two in the field. (Your teachers or your parents might help you think of someone.) If so, you should look ahead toward your interview as you do your reading and note taking—the more you know, the better your questions can be. After you have your questions planned, you can make an appointment for the interview.

When you go to the interview, take along a small tape recorder and ask permission to record the conversation for your own use only. Do not depend entirely on the tape, however; during the interview go ahead and jot down brief answers to your questions. Your interviewee will appreciate your being well organized and considerate of his or her time. Afterward, remember to write a thank-you note promptly.

Read and Take Notes

When you have located some good sources, you can begin reading and taking notes. You need to take content notes to help you remember what you learn and where you learned it. And you need to keep track of essential information about your sources so that you will not have to locate them again to find out, for example, where and when they were published.

Traditionally, the content notes are written on four-by-six-inch note cards, and the facts about sources are written on three-by-five-inch bibliography cards. Although that system works well, you can also use a word processor (usually on a personal computer) for recording both kinds of information.

The information about the sources you are using is called your **working bibliography.** Physically, it usually exists on a series of three-by-five-inch bibliography cards. Each card has on it the necessary information about one source you are using. The cards, of course, are easily alphabetized and carried.

Never take notes from a source without making a bibliography card for it—it would be a great waste of time to go back to look up the source information again. Besides, if the source is a book, someone else might have checked it out of the library by the time you return.

You will also save time by writing down the source information in the form you will need to use later. For example, you will write down a book's author (last name first), exact title, and facts of publication (city, publisher, and date). Follow your teacher's instructions on which forms to use and refer to either "MLA Style for Documenting Sources" (Chapter 2) or "Documenting Sources in the Sciences" (Chapter 4). For your own convenience, you can also write down the call number for each library book.

You can accomplish the same purposes on a word processor, especially if you have a laptop computer that is easily carried to the library. Make a file for your working bibliography and enter the information for your sources. Whenever you need to add, delete, or change an entry, open the file and make the changes, saving the revised file for future use. You can also rearrange the bibliography file to put your sources in alphabetical order. Whenever you need to, you can print a copy of the file to review or take to the library. In fact, you are wise to print a copy periodically as a backup in addition to making disk backups for safety.

Whether you use cards or a computer file, your working bibliography will eventually develop into the list of sources (or references) at the end of your paper.

Content notes are conveniently taken on four-by-six-inch **note cards** (or perhaps in subtopic files on a laptop computer). Here is where you write down the relevant information you find. At the top of each note card (or computer file) write a **slug,** a brief phrase telling its contents. If you have already written a tentative outline, try to use the points on the outline as slugs on your note cards.

Each time you take notes from a source, be sure to identify clearly which source and which pages you are using. You can identify the source by title and author or by a temporary numbering system, using a different number for each source.

There are three basic methods of note taking: summary, brief phrases (to help you paraphrase), and quotation. Most notes should be in your own words—either summary or brief phrases—because you are looking for information, not someone else's wording.

When you need only the general idea from a passage, just summarize it. That is, for a long paragraph or two you might write down just one sentence to capture the general idea. Try to express your summary entirely in your own words. If you do use a phrase from the source, be sure to copy it accurately and enclose it in quotation marks. Also record page numbers carefully, both for facts and for quotations.

When you need specific facts from a passage, the best method is to write them down in brief phrases. Later, when you use the note card in writing your paper, you will be able to see the facts easily. You will also have greater freedom to write them up in a way that will naturally fit in with the flow of your paper. As you take notes in brief phrases, try to express them in your own way. Here too, if you do use a phrase from the source, be sure to place quotation marks around it. Also make clear on your card what part of the information comes from which page; you may end up using just part of the information that you obtained from two or more pages.

Direct quotations from a source are not often needed. Of course, it is appropriate to quote brief passages of a literary work you are analyzing; see examples (from *The Red Badge of Courage*) on page 19. If you are writing a paper that is not a literary analysis, you might once or twice in the paper quote a source sentence for emphasis or because of its special effectiveness.

When you do quote, copy the sentence or phrase exactly—words, spelling, and punctuation. Remember to put those words in quotation marks. If you later need to change anything so that the quotation will fit into your sentence or paragraph, use square brackets for an addition or substitution, as illustrated in the second example from *The Red Badge of Courage*. Omitted words are indicated by ellipsis marks, three spaced dots (. . .).

Anyone writing a research paper makes use of some facts or ideas that he found in doing his research. In this important stage of your research, you are trying to take notes complete enough to answer all your questions or to support all the subtopics on your tentative outline. At the same time you need to be careful to avoid **plagiarism.** Plagiarism is intentional or unintentional dishonesty with your sources. Unless a fact is **common knowledge**—something mentioned by nearly everyone who writes about the subject—you should tell where you learned it.

You can avoid plagiarism by being careful to credit the facts and ideas that you get from others and by using quotation marks as part of crediting the wording you get from others. When you paraphrase (put something into your own words), be sure to do so completely—use your own words, your own sentence structure, and your own ordering of ideas.

Below are examples of acceptable and unacceptable paraphrase.

- **The original material—**

    Niagara Falls actually consists of two waterfalls, the Horseshoe Falls and the American Falls. The Horseshoe Falls is on the Canadian side of the border in the province of Ontario. The American Falls is on the United States side in the state of New York.

    (Macinko, George. "Niagara Falls." *The World Book Encyclopedia.* 1994.)

- **Acceptable paraphrase (change in words and structure)—**

    The Horseshoe Falls in Ontario and the American Falls in New York make up Niagara Falls.

- **Unacceptable paraphrase (plagiarism of words and structure underlined)—**

    <u>Niagara Falls actually consists of</u> more than one waterfall. <u>On the Canadian side of the border</u> is the Horseshoe Falls and <u>on the United States side</u> is the American Falls.

- **Acceptable paraphrase of part and quoting of part—**

    Niagara Falls, which "consists of two waterfalls, the Horseshoe Falls and the American Falls," spans the border between Ontario and New York.

Later you will learn how to give credit. For now, as you take notes, just keep track of the facts—the sources, the pages, and the quotation marks needed.

Organize

As you progress toward the end of your reading and note taking, work on organizing your information. Use the slugs to group your note cards together according to their contents. (If you took notes in computer files with slugs at the top, print out those files.) Now arrange your note-card groups (or computer printouts) and think about the organization of the paper as a whole. If you made a tentative outline earlier, does it still look workable? If you did not, or if changes are needed, make a logical outline now.

Do you have enough information to support all the parts your paper needs? If not, look for the missing information. You may need to find a few more sources, or possibly you can look further in the ones you have.

This is also a good time to write a thesis statement for your paper. The thesis is the sentence that expresses the main idea of your paper. It includes the topic and your point of view about the topic. For example, the thesis of this section on organization might be stated as follows: "A clear sense of organization helps writers collect all the information they need and gives them direction in the process of writing."

Look at the following three possible thesis statements and decide which one you think is best. Do you see any problems with the other two?

1. In this paper I will tell about the construction machinery used to prepare a building site.
2. Preparing land and constructing a tall building are complicated jobs.
3. The construction machinery used to prepare a building site performs three functions.

The first statement announces the topic, but it does not state the main idea of the paper. Also notice that its subject *I* and verb *will tell* speak about the writer rather than stating the main idea. (Keep yourself out of the thesis statement.) The second statement announces a main idea, but it is much too broad—that idea could be covered in a book but not in a research paper. The third statement is a workable thesis. It states a main idea, and it is not too broad to cover. Although it does not have to, it even suggests the organization of the paper.

When you have a satisfactory thesis for your paper, reconsider your outline—does everything in the outline directly or indirectly support the thesis? If not, drop or change some points in the outline. Do not keep something in the paper just because you have notes on it; anything that does not serve a good purpose will work against the unity and effectiveness of your paper.

When you have a good grasp of the purpose and structure of your paper, and when you have all the information you need to support that structure, you are ready to write.

Write the First Draft

With your thesis, outline, and organized notes at hand, you can sit down and write the first draft, perhaps saving your introduction to write last. One caution, however: do not let your notes control your writing. Remember that this is *your* paper, and your thinking is primary. So present your thinking, using your information to back it up.

Try to find a time and place that will allow you to write the entire first draft in one session. If you cannot do that, look for several large chunks of time fairly close together. Each time you sit down to write, review your thesis and your outline. If you have already written part of the paper, reread the last few paragraphs to give you a running start. Then consult the relevant notes and start writing.

If you have access to a personal computer or other word processor, use it for writing your paper. Once you learn the system, you can easily revise and correct what you have written. You save the revised version, which you can retrieve for further improvements or additions later. At any point, you can print out the current version. Be sure to save your document often; also, make backup copies on a disk for safekeeping. For example, you can save your work every fifteen minutes and make a backup copy at the end of every work session.

If you do not have a computer available but you do have a typewriter, learn to do your writing at the typewriter. For a first draft, you need not worry about hitting wrong keys. After you develop some speed, typing is much faster than writing by hand—and it is much easier to read. Type double-spaced, with at least one-inch margins; you want plenty of room to revise conveniently. Whether you write or type, use just one side of the paper. If nothing is on the backs of pages, you can see everything at once, and you can even cut up pages if you need to rearrange some ideas.

If your notes are mostly summaries and brief phrases written in your own words, you should have no problem writing the paper mostly in your own words. Remember to use the source's wording only for some special purpose, and be sure to use quotation marks if you do quote a phrase or a sentence. As you write, carefully record the source and page numbers from each note card you use. (Review the paragraphs on pages 9-10 about plagiarism.)

Different writers have different work methods. Many prefer to work fast until the first draft is complete. Others write more slowly and carefully. Still others prefer to work fairly steadily during a single work session; then (perhaps after lunch) they reread and partly revise the last session's work before going on into new territory. Students too should write in the way that works best for them.

If you find yourself at a dead end, try thinking through your thesis and your outline again. Imagine someone listening to you. Now that you have told the person the part you last wrote, what do you want to say next? If you are not sure how to say it, just write down *something*.

Later you can come back and make it sound better. Your goal now is to get your flow back, to keep going.

When you finish the rest of the paper, go back to write the introduction paragraph. Consider it a funnel that starts big and gradually narrows down to your thesis statement. Start with a broad area of interest to your readers, and then lead them in to your target. The thesis statement should be either the last sentence or the main clause of the last sentence. Can you find the thesis in this example?

> Everyone likes to watch the construction of a large project. People who drive by the same construction site day after day often wonder why it seems to take months for anything to get out of the ground. Week after week, large bulldozers and other heavy machinery move around, but nothing seems to happen. Then at last the walls start to go up, and progress is obvious. Although few people realize the importance of preparing the site for a large construction project, site-preparation machinery performs three vital functions.

The thesis statement is the main clause of the last sentence: "site-preparation machinery performs three vital functions." The next paragraph will begin the body by describing the first function and how it is carried out.

Rethink, Revise, and Edit

Regardless of how quickly or how carefully you wrote the first draft, you can improve it by rereading and then revising it. Even professionals revise their writing.

The first step in revision is to let your paper rest for a day or two. Then when you come back to it, you will be able to see it more as others will. If you wrote it on a word processor, print it out so that you can see more at one time; and print it double-spaced so that you can easily mark on it.

As you go through the paper, try to read it as if you have never seen it before. Probably you will notice some parts that are unclear or awkward, some that are unnecessarily repetitive, and perhaps some that are incomplete. You might simply mark problems in the margin and keep on reading. Then go back and use pencil to improve the problem areas. If a sentence or a section seems irrelevant, or perhaps unimportant and uninteresting, consider whether it really supports your thesis. If not, do not hesitate to drop it. Also eliminate unnecessary repetition.

If part or all of your handwritten or typed copy gets so full of changes that it is hard to read, write or type a new copy. You will probably improve it somewhat just in copying it, and the new copy will help you read it smoothly in order to catch any other needed changes. Your later editing should include supplying smooth transitions and correcting errors of grammar and mechanics, including spelling and punctuation.

If you are using a word processor, work from your marked paper copy to make needed changes in the electronic document. Feel free to make other changes directly in the file. (Remember to save and back up the new version.) Then print out another paper copy. Let it rest, and then read it fresh again; edit and make further changes as needed.

If your word processor has a spelling checker, use it but do not depend on it. It might not recognize a correctly spelled word, and it will approve a misspelled word that happens to be another word (such as *the* for *they* or homonyms such as *break* for *brake*). For the first problem, check with a standard desk dictionary; and for the second, do your own proofreading too. Grammar or usage checkers have the same kinds of problems—nothing electronic can be an adequate substitute for your own careful reading and editing.

Complete the Paper

Now that the words are right, you can finish the paper. The easiest part is the **title page,** which should be prepared (or omitted) according to your teacher's instructions. Usually the title is centered on the whole page with normal title capitalization (not in all caps or underlined or in quotation marks). Then in the lower right corner, within the normal one-inch margins and on separate double-spaced lines, are these four items: your name, your teacher's name, the course name (and section if needed), and the date submitted.

Another style of title page centers everything. The centered title is about a third of the way down the page, and then your centered name is about four double spaces down. On the last three double-spaced lines before the one-inch bottom margin are the remaining three centered items (teacher, course, date).

When a title page is used, the centered title is repeated one inch from the top of the first page of the body of the paper. The text begins on the following double-spaced line.

If your teacher does not require a title page, the four double-spaced items (your name, teacher, course, date) can go in the upper left of page 1 within the normal one-inch margins. Then the title (in the same form as described above) is centered on the next double-spaced line. The text begins on the following double-spaced line.

You may be asked to include your **outline** in your paper. (If so, you do need a title page.) If you kept your outline current as you planned and wrote, it should be fairly easy to put into final form. Be sure to use letters and numerals in the standard sequence: roman numerals for main divisions, capital letters for subdivisions, and arabic numerals if you have lesser subdivisions (I. A. 1.). Unless you are writing a sentence outline, you should use phrases only, and equal elements should be parallel grammatically. You can use all noun phrases or mostly noun phrases with perhaps a section of gerunds (verbs with *-ing* endings) or adjectives.

The outline page follows the title page and is completely double-spaced. The word *Outline* is centered one inch below the top of the page. Like the other headings in the paper, it has no underlines and no quotation marks. According to the length of your outline, you can begin typing the outline either one or two double spaces down from the heading.

The final step is to put the source references into final form—both the **citations** in the text and the **list of sources** at the end.

If you are using MLA style (published by The Modern Language Association), first make sure you have correct form for your parenthetical citations in the text (see pages 17-21). Then turn your working bibliography into the alphabetical list of works cited. See Chapter 2 for information on checking the forms and typing the reference list.

If you are using CBE style (produced by the Council of Biology Editors) for a science paper, you will probably use consecutive numbers as parenthetical or superscript citations in the text (see pages 43-44). On the latest draft of your text, use a distinctive color to assign these numbers now. In the same color, write matching numbers by the appropriate sources in your working bibliography. Arrange the sources in numerical order, and check their forms with the information in Chapter 4. See the reference list section in Chapter 4 for instructions on typing the reference list.

If you are using a word processor, make any needed changes in the text, such as adding or adjusting parenthetical citations.

Make the Final Copy

If you are not using a word processor, now is the time to type your final copy. Be sure to leave a one-inch margin on all sides, double-space everything, and use only one side of the paper. The same requirements apply if you are allowed to write the paper by hand; be sure to write legibly in dark blue or black ink. Similarly, the typewriter ribbon needs to produce clear, dark type. After completing the final copy, proofread it carefully. Be neat in making any needed minor corrections. If you need to, retype a page.

On a word processor, you can print out a semifinal copy to proofread. Also be sure the program is set to print double-spaced with one-inch margins, but do not justify the lines of type. Use a normal-sized legible print style rather than something fancy. Also be sure your printer cartridge or ribbon is in good condition to give clear, dark print. Make any needed corrections or adjustments and print the final copy.

Now assemble the pages in the correct order: title page (if any), outline page (if any), body of the paper (pages in order), notes page (if any), and works cited or references page. Unless your teacher has given you other instructions, simply staple the paper securely in the upper left corner.

CHAPTER 2

MLA Style for Documenting Sources

In literature and languages particularly, and in other humanities as well, the system most used for documenting sources is the MLA system, published by the Modern Language Association. MLA style for research papers is based on Joseph Gibaldi, *MLA Handbook for Writers of Research Papers,* 4th ed. (New York: Modern Language Association, 1995).

Since 1984, MLA style has provided the widely used option of brief parenthetical source citations in the text, rather than source footnotes (used at the bottom of each page) or endnotes (used at the end of the paper). The parenthetical citations identify the source in the briefest possible way (simply by author when possible) and also specify the relevant page or pages. The alphabetic list of works cited gives the full information about each source. This book follows the current *MLA Handbook* in recommending parenthetical citations.

Parenthetical Citations in the Text

Basics

In MLA style, sources are cited in the body of the paper by brief parenthetical notes such as the one in this sentence:

> During the Viking Age, the town of Hedeby in southern Jutland was one of the primary centers of luxury trade for all of northern Europe (Magnusson 68-69).

This parenthetical citation tells the reader that the information about Hedeby came from pages 68 and 69 in a work by Magnusson. To learn more about this work, the reader can turn to the list of works cited and find the following information.

> Magnusson, Magnus. Vikings! New York: Dutton, 1980.

The entry states that Magnus Magnusson wrote the book titled *Vikings!* and that it was published in New York by E. P. Dutton in 1980. The book title here is underlined to represent italics. Further examples in this section use italics.

Parenthetical citations must clearly identify specific sources. If you use two or more works by the same author, add the title (either shortened or complete) after the author's name and a comma:

> Luxury goods came through Hedeby from all directions (Magnusson, *Vikings!* 69).

However, you should keep parenthetical references as brief as possible by not repeating information that is already in the sentence. For example, if you mention the author's name or other information in the sentence, do not repeat it in the parenthetical citation.

> In *Vikings!* Magnusson names some of the luxury goods that "flowed through the town" of Hedeby (69).

> Magnusson describes Viking forays into the new world in *Viking Expansion Westwards.*

In the second reference no parenthetical documentation is needed. Author and title are already present; and because the whole book is being cited, no page numbers are necessary.

If you wish to include more than one source in a single parenthetical reference, you may do so by separating the sources with a semicolon.

> Much is known about the houses of Hedeby (Dirksen 323; Magnusson, *Vikings!* 69).

If, however, the parenthetical reference would create a long interruption, you would be wise to cite the multiple sources as a supplementary note. (See page 21.)

Placement

The *MLA Handbook* recommends that you place the parenthetical citation at the end of the sentence or at a natural pause in the sentence, keeping it as close as possible to the material being acknowledged. The parenthetical citation comes *before* the punctuation needed at that spot in the sentence.

> Other scholars, such as Windhurst (2: 59-60), disagree with this conclusion.

> Other scholars disagree with this conclusion (e.g., Windhurst 2: 59-60).

> In Lorimer's translation of the New Testament into Scots, "only the Devil speaks Standard English" (McCrum, Cran, and MacNeil 145).

> Is it surprising that in Appalachia the remote dialects are believed to be more pure (Scogdill et al. 13-14, 17)?

The first two references, citing Volume 2 of Windhurst, show the usual placement of a parenthetical citation before a comma or a period.

The third illustrates closing quotation marks *before* the parenthetical citation; the sentence-closing period comes *after* the parenthetical citation. The fourth illustrates the final question mark, as well as *et al.* (Latin for "and others"), used when a work has more than three authors.

If you need to quote a prose excerpt of more than four typed lines (or more than three lines of poetry), the entire quotation is indented one inch—ten pica spaces or twelve elite spaces on a typewriter—and no quotation marks are added. In this case the parenthetical citation comes after the closing punctuation and a blank space; no punctuation follows it.

> One problematic matter in interpreting *The Red Badge of Courage* is whether to take at face value Henry's estimate of his own maturing:
>
>> With this conviction came a store of assurance. He felt a quiet manhood, nonassertive but of sturdy and strong blood. He knew that he would no more quail before his guides wherever they should point. He had been to touch the great death, and found that, after all, it was but the great death. He was a man. (99)

Special matters

Sometimes you need to do something out of the ordinary in order to identify the location within the work or to identify the work itself.

If a literary work is available in multiple editions, you can help your reader by giving more than just a page number. For example, for a book you can give the chapter; or for a play you can give the act, scene, and lines.

> At the end of *The Red Badge of Courage,* Henry acquires "a store of assurance" and feels that "he [is] a man" (99; ch. 24).

Also, notice here the square brackets for a substitution or addition to a quotation. No introductory comma and no beginning capitalization are needed when you integrate a quoted phrase or sentence into your own sentence.

If your source (perhaps an electronic journal) uses paragraph numbers instead of page numbers, give the necessary information using the abbreviation *par.* or *pars.* If the author's name appears, it is followed by a comma.

> Overmanaging a stock portfolio is both expensive and foolish (Harter, par. 16).

If your source names no author, identify the source by its title. You can shorten the title, but be sure to include its first word so that it can be located alphabetically in the list of sources.

Word processing programs commonly include many equation symbols (e.g., *WordPerfect Reference* 715-17).

Note that inclusive numbers are stated in MLA style by giving the last two digits of the second number (715-17), unless more digits are necessary: 97-103, 107-09, 198-203, 1349-421. Years also follow this rule unless they are in different centuries: 1891-92, 1896-1902.

If an organization is named as the author, use that name. If the name is long, it will be less of an interruption if it appears in the sentence itself, as in the second example below.

Several characteristics can indicate high quality in a doctoral nursing program (American Association of Colleges of Nursing 200).

According to the American Association of Colleges of Nursing, several characteristics can indicate high quality in doctoral nursing programs (200).

When you parenthetically cite an editor (perhaps quoting from the editor's introduction to an edited work), simply give the editor's name without the abbreviation *ed.* The list of works cited, which comes at the end of the paper, will clarify his role as editor.

If you repeatedly quote a well-known literary work, you may use its common abbreviation in parenthetical citations. Examples are *Ham.* for *Hamlet, RB* for *The Red Badge of Courage,* and *GT* for *Gulliver's Travels.* It is usually best to introduce the abbreviation the first time you refer to the work.

In *Julius Caesar (JC),* Shakespeare creates a work of art from historical events.

Then use that abbreviation when you refer to act, scene, and lines: "(*JC* 3.1.1-3)."

Similarly, in parenthetical citations, you may use the common three- or four-letter abbreviations of books of the Bible whose names are longer than four letters (e.g., Gen., Exod., Matt., Gal., Phil., Philem.).

The song of Moses (Exod. 15:1-19) will be sung in heaven (Rev. 15:3).

John the Baptist again said, "Behold the Lamb of God!" (John 1:36).

These references call for one work-cited entry: The Bible. King James Version. (no underlines, no facts of publication)

Normally you quote original sources, not someone else telling about the original. If you do need to cite an indirect source, use the abbreviation *qtd. in* for "quoted in."

> Crane wrote to the *Newark Sunday Call* that his ancestors had been
> "pretty hot people" in New Jersey (qtd. in Cady 30).

Notes for Supplementary Information

Even though you use parenthetical documentation, you may still use footnotes or endnotes for supplementary information that would interrupt the body of the paper. There are two types of possible supplementary notes: content notes and reference notes.

Content notes can clarify or support what you have written in the body of the paper. Be careful here—usually such information is either important enough to include in the text itself or unimportant enough to leave out. Use a note only if the material is important but would interrupt the flow of your explanation or argument.

Reference notes can give evaluative comments about sources, such as their bias or accuracy. Reference notes can also cite multiple sources, enabling you to avoid interrupting your sentence or paragraph with a long string of names and pages.

If you use a supplementary note, link it to the sentence or phrase in the text by using a superscript number. The note itself follows a matching superscript number at the bottom of the page (for a footnote) or at the end of the text (for an endnote). The first line of a note is indented one-half inch (five pica spaces or six elite spaces on a typewriter), and the following lines come to the left margin.

Endnotes begin a new page just after the body of the paper with the centered heading *Note* or *Notes* typed an inch from the top of the page. The heading has no underline and no quotation marks. Everything is double-spaced: the body of the paper, the headings, the endnotes, and the list of works cited. (Only footnotes are single-spaced, with a double space between them; but few papers today contain footnotes.) Here is an example of an endnote.

> [1] The description of *blue-clothed* indicates that these are Union
> troops: the Confederates wear gray or butternut.

The List of Works Cited

The final section of your paper is the alphabetical list of works cited. The works cited are the works from which you have acknowledged taking some information or wording for use in your paper. That is, these are the works to which you have referred at least once in a parenthetical citation in the body of your paper.

The list begins on a new page with the centered heading *Works Cited* one inch from the top of the page. As on the Notes page, the first double-spaced entry is two spaces below the heading. Each entry begins at the left margin, and any following lines are indented one-half inch, or five pica or six elite spaces on a typewriter. This arrangement makes it easy to search for a source alphabetically.

Other possible titles for your list of works are *Bibliography* and *Selected Bibliography,* but neither of these titles is completely clear about just what is included. The title *Works Cited* includes everything you cited and excludes anything you did not. If your teacher approves, however, you may expand your list to include works that were helpful to you but from which you took no specific information; in that case your list would be called *Works Consulted.*

The author's name should appear in full as it is in the work. The author's (or first author's) last name comes first for the purpose of alphabetizing. When alphabetizing by the authors' names, ignore first names unless the last names are identical.

Johns, Jasper

Johnson, Thomas A.

Also ignore spaces and punctuation within last names.

Dali, Salvador

D'Allessio, Angelo

Two works coauthored by the same person are further alphabetized by the second authors' last names.

Masters, Joyce, and Richard Larkey

Masters, Joyce, and Andrea F. Thompson

When no author is known, alphabetize by the title, ignoring beginning articles (a, an, the). For example, *A Complete Guide to Sewing* would appear under *C* rather than *A*.

If two or more works have the same author, give the name in the first entry only. After that, use three hyphens followed by a period. However, if the person was an editor, translator, or compiler, use a comma instead of a period and follow it with the appropriate abbreviation.

Smith, Carole. *Five Twentieth-Century Poets.* Austin: U of Texas P, 1985.

——, ed. *Robert Frost: Early Critical Essays.* Boston: Little, 1979.

——. *T. S. Eliot's Christian Symbolism.* New York: Barnhart, 1995.

Works by the same author are alphabetized by title.

Underlining is the typed equivalent of italic print. Underlining or italic print is needed for the titles of books, periodicals, and other independent publications. If your computer or typewriter is able to produce italics, use them; otherwise underline. This book uses underlining in the general patterns and italics in the specific examples.

Books

The forms in this section apply also to booklets and pamphlets.

The facts of publication include city, publisher, and date. If more than one city is listed in the book, give only the first. Normally you can use just the city without the state. If the city is outside the United States and its location could be unclear, for Canada give the province abbreviation and for other countries abbreviate the name of the country: Winnipeg, MB; Cambridge, Eng.; Tokyo.

The names of publishers are shortened to the primary word *(Dutton for E. P. Dutton)* or to the first name in a series *(Prentice for Prentice Hall, Harcourt for Harcourt Brace Jovanovich).* Omit unnecessary words such as *Publishers, Inc.,* and *Press;* but use *UP* for *University Press.* Also use *U* for *University.*

For reference, here is the ordering when extra information is needed for a book.

Author; title of book part; title of book; name of editor, translator, or compiler; edition used; number of volumes or of volume used; name of the series; city, publisher, and date of publication; inclusive pages of the book part; any additional information or annotation.

General pattern for a book

Author(s). Title. Place of publication: publisher name, year.

• Book by one author; subtitle after a colon

Hirsch, E. D., Jr. *Cultural Literacy: What Every American Needs to Know.* Boston: Houghton, 1987. [The author's name is given as on the title page. Missing information may be filled in, using square brackets: Hirsch, E[ric] D[onald], Jr.]

- **More than one author**

McCrum, Robert, William Cran, and Robert MacNeil. *The Story of English.* New York: Viking, 1986.

- **More than three authors (alternate forms)**

Quirk, Randolph, Sidney Greenbaum, Geoffrey Leech, and Jan Svartik. *A Comprehensive Grammar of the English Language.* London: Longman, 1985.

Quirk, Randolph, et al. *A Comprehensive Grammar of the English Language.* London: Longman, 1985.

- **Edition number**

Troyka, Lynn Quitman. *Simon and Schuster Handbook for Writers.* 3rd ed. Englewood Cliffs: Prentice, 1993.

- **Organization as author**

Council of Biology Editors. *Scientific Style and Format: The CBE Manual for Authors, Editors, and Publishers.* 6th ed. New York: Cambridge UP, 1994.

- **Publisher's imprint**

Goldberg, Jeff. *Anatomy of a Scientific Discovery.* New York: Bantam-Doubleday, 1988. [Bantam Books is one of the imprints, or special group names, used by Doubleday; and so the imprint and the publisher are joined by a hyphen.]

- **Volume in a series**

Cady, Edwin H. *Stephen Crane.* Rev. ed. Twayne's United States Authors Ser. 23. Boston: Twayne-Hall, 1980. [Revised edition. Volume 23 in the series. Twayne Publishers is a division or imprint of G. K. Hall.]

- **No author or editor given (alphabetized by title)**

Merriam-Webster's Collegiate Thesaurus. Springfield, MA: Merriam, 1988.

- **Editor, compiler, or translator (ed., comp., trans.)**

Vins, Georgi, comp. *Let the Waters Roar: Evangelists in the Gulag.* Grand Rapids: Baker, 1989.

- **Introduction, preface, foreword, or afterword**

Vins, Georgi. Introduction. *Let the Waters Roar: Evangelists in the Gulag.* Grand Rapids: Baker, 1989. 9-11. [If front matter is paged in small roman numerals, use that form: ix-xi.]

- **Article in an edited or compiled book**

Rytikov, Vladimir. "Cellmate of a False Christ." *Let the Waters Roar: Evangelists in the Gulag.* Comp. Georgi Vins. Grand Rapids: Baker, 1989. 53-66. [inclusive page numbers for the article]

- **Unsigned article in a familiar reference book**

"Iodoform." *Merriam-Webster's Collegiate Dictionary.* 10th ed. 1993. [Familiar reference works are identified only by edition and year; for others give full publication information. If articles are arranged alphabetically, omit the volume and page numbers.]

- **Signed article in a familiar reference book**

Chemla, Karine Carole. "Mathematics in China and Japan." In "Mathematics, The History of." *The New Encyclopaedia Britannica: Macropaedia.* 15th ed. 1997. [Chemla wrote the section about Chinese and Japanese mathematics, which is within the article on the history of mathematics, alphabetized under *M.* Normally one article is named and *in* is not used.]

- **Previously published article reprinted in a collection**

Hungerford, Harold R. " 'That Was at Chancellorsville': The Factual Framework of *The Red Badge of Courage.*" *American Literature* 34 (1963): 520-31. Rpt. in *Stephen Crane's Career: Perspectives and Evaluations.* Ed. Thomas A. Gullason. New York: New York UP, 1972. 205-16.

- **Republished book**

Andrews, Samuel J. *Christianity and Anti-Christianity in Their Final Conflict.* 1898. Greenville, SC: Bob Jones UP, 1991.

- **Missing information**

Henderson, G.F.R. *Stonewall Jackson and the American Civil War.* New York: Grosset, n.d. [Besides *n.d.* for "no date," other abbreviations are *n.p.,* used when there is no place of publication (used before the colon) or no publisher given (used after the

colon), and *N. pag.* for "No pagination," used at the end of the
entry to explain why citations lack page numbers.]

- **Multivolume work, using two or more volumes**

Lewis, Meriwether, and William Clark. *The History of the Lewis and
Clark Expedition.* Ed. Elliott Coues. 1893. 3 vols. New York:
Dover, n.d. [The reprint has no date.]

- **Multivolume work, using one volume only**

Lewis, Meriwether, and William Clark. *The History of the Lewis and
Clark Expedition.* Ed. Elliott Coues. 1893. Vol. 2. New York:
Dover, n.d. [Because you have given the volume number, your
parenthetical citations in the text need give only page numbers.]

- **Government publication, with and without author**

Hodge, Carleton T., and Ibrahim Umaru. *Hausa: Basic Course.* US
Department of State. Foreign Service Institute Basic Course
Series. Washington: GPO, 1963. [*GPO* represents the
Government Printing Office, the publisher of most federal
publications.]

United States. Cong. Joint Committee on the Investigation of the Pearl
Harbor Attack. *Hearings.* 79th Cong., 1st and 2nd sess. 32 vols.
Washington: GPO, 1946. [The ordering before the title is from
greater to smaller divisions: the United States government, the
Congress, the Joint Committee.]

Scholarly Journals

Scholarly journals are intended for professionals and college
students. But because their articles contain original scholarly work
(research and interpretations), they can be an important resource for a
high school student. Usually a scholarly journal does not appear as
many times a year as a magazine for the general public. Many journals
are paged consecutively for the entire year.

General pattern for a journal article

Author(s). "Article title." <u>Journal title</u> volume.issue-if-paged-by-issue
(year): inclusive pages.

- **Journal article**

Hungerford, Harold R. " 'That Was at Chancellorsville': The Factual
    Framework of *The Red Badge of Courage.*" *American Literature*
    34 (1963): 520-31.

- **More than three authors**

Berg, William P., et al. "Correlates of Recurrent Falling in Inde-
    pendent Community-Dwelling Older Adults." *Journal of Motor
    Behavior* 29 (1997): 5-16.

- **Author not stated in the source**

"Manuscript Preparation Guidelines." *Journal of Radio Studies*
    4 (1997): 310-11.

- **Article in a journal paged by issue**

Hamilton, Jill. "Encouraging Student Writers: Reversing Roles in
    Senior Composition." *English Journal* 86.1 (1997): 51-54.
    [volume 86, number 1]

Other Periodicals

For newspapers and weekly or biweekly magazines, give the
complete date (day month year). Abbreviate the names of all months
over four letters long. Do not give the volume and issue numbers of a
magazine.

For a newspaper with lettered sections, use the section letter with
the page number: B5. If the article is continued on a nonconsecutive
page such as page 9, simply use a plus sign: B5+. Also use the plus sign
for a magazine article not printed on consecutive pages.

General patterns for newspaper and magazine articles

Author(s). "Article Title." <u>Newspaper title</u> date: page(s).
Author(s). "Article Title." <u>Newspaper title</u> date, edition: page(s).
Author(s). "Article Title." <u>Magazine title</u> date: inclusive pages.

- **Newspaper article**

Pipp, Tracy L. "Do-It-Yourself Projects Can Aggravate Allergies."
    Greenville News [SC] 31 July 1997, final ed.: B1.

- **Unsigned newspaper article**

"New Drug Helps in Treating Arthritis." *Indianapolis Star* 17 July
    1997: A7.

- **Letter to the editor**

Knowles, Gail. Letter. *Greenville News* [SC] 30 July 1997, final ed.:
    A10.

- **Magazine article**

Naitram, Carl. "The Letter: Special Delivery Providence." *Frontline*
    July-Aug. 1997: 12-13.

- **Magazine editorial**

Bell, Rod. "Emotion That Acts." Editorial. *Frontline* July-Aug. 1997:
    4. [A newspaper editorial is done similarly, with the word
    Editorial after its title.]

Electronic Publications

Electronic publications include sources that you find by researching
on a computer. This section explains how to acknowledge your
software and online sources. The basic patterns are from the *MLA
Handbook,* slightly updated and expanded in line with current
technology and practices.

The general patterns should cover most situations. However, in
certain electronic communications you may find that the relevant facts
differ from the general pattern. In that case, use the various patterns to
help you figure out a similar way to state the facts. For example,
because page numbers from a book part come after the book title and
publication facts, by analogy the item number for a database record can
be placed after the database title. See the federal budget example on
page 30.

The following patterns for online sources call for "protocol and
address with access path." (The protocol is the electronic language
used.) An example is http://www.merck.com/pubs/mmanual/ for *The
Merck Manual of Diagnosis and Therapy,* referenced on the next page.
In it, *http* is the protocol, *www.merck.com* is the electronic address, and
the remainder is the access path to follow to find this electronic book.
Note that this string of symbols does *not* end with a period when you
use it on the Internet. In the works-cited entry, a period is added
because all the separate parts of an entry end with a period.

General patterns for electronic-journal articles and electronic books

Author(s). "Article title." <u>Journal, newsletter, or conference title</u>
    volume.issue-or-file-number (date): number of pages or
    paragraphs or *n. pag.* for "no pagination." Publication medium
    (*Online*). Protocol and address with access path. Date accessed.
Author(s). <u>Book title</u>. Version or edition number if applicable. Place:
    publisher, year (when updated if applicable). Online. Protocol
    and address with access path. Date accessed.

• Electronic-journal article

Garbin, Lidia. *"The Fortunes of Perkin Warbeck:* Walter Scott in the
    Writings of Mary Shelley." *Romanticism on the Net* issue 6 (May
    1997): n. pag. Online. http://users.ox.ac.uk/~scat0385/
    warbeck.html. 5 Aug. 1997.

• Electronic book

The Merck Manual of Diagnosis and Therapy. 16th ed. Whitehouse
    Station, NJ: Merck, 1992. Internet version. Merck, 1997. Online.
    http://www.merck.com/pubs/mmanual/. 5 Aug. 1997.

• Article in an electronic book

"Hemorrhagic Disorders." *The Merck Manual of Diagnosis and
    Therapy.* 16th ed. Whitehouse Station, NJ: Merck, 1992. Internet
    version. Merck, 1997. Article no. 96. Online.
    http://www.merck.com/pubs/mmanual/. 5 Aug. 1997.

General pattern for public online postings (newsgroups, bulletin boards, forums, etc.)

Author(s). "Title of posting." Date posted. Online posting. Newsgroup
    or forum. Date accessed.

• Public online posting

Retorio, Anthony. "The Last Will and Testament of Geoffrey of
    Anjou." 4 Aug. 1997. Online posting. Usenet: soc.history. 5 Aug.
    1997.

General pattern for electronic texts of literary and historical documents

Author(s). <u>Title of the text</u>. Publication information for the printed source. Online. Institution holding the electronic text. Protocol and address with access path. Date accessed.

• Electronic text of literary document

Shakespeare, William. *Macbeth. The Complete Works of William Shakespeare.* [1623]. Online. MIT. http://the-tech.mit.edu/ Shakespeare/works.html. 5 Aug. 1997.

Crane, Stephen. *The Red Badge of Courage.* [1895]. Online. The Project Gutenberg Etext of *The Red Badge of Courage,* 1996. Etext no. 463. ftp://uiarchive.cso.uiuc.edu/pub/etext/gutenberg/ etext96/badge10a.txt. 5 Aug. 1997.

General pattern for print-source material accessed from an on-line database

Author(s). Title and full publication information for the printed source. <u>Database title</u>. Online. Name of the computer service if any. Protocol and address with access path. Date accessed.

• Print-source article accessed from an online database

Wilson, David L. "Striking Back at 'Spamming' on the Net." *San Jose Mercury News* 4 Aug. 1997: n. pag. *Mercury Center.* 5 Aug. 1997. Online. http://www.sjmercury.com/business/ uunet080497.htm. 5 Aug. 1997. [It was published in the newspaper on August 4 and online on August 5.]

General pattern for material from online database (no printed source or analogue)

Author(s). "Title of material accessed." Date if given. <u>Database title</u>. Online. Name of the computer service if any. Protocol and address with access path. Date accessed.

• Information from online database, no print source evident

"Federal Budget—Summary." 1996. *Statistical Abstract of the United States.* No. 512. Online. http://www.census.gov/statab/freq/ 96s0512.txt. 5 Aug. 1997.

General pattern for print-source material from a periodical portable database (CD-ROM, diskette, magnetic tape)

Author(s). Title and full publication information for the printed source. <u>Database title</u>. Publication medium (CD-ROM, diskette, or magnetic tape). Name of vendor if relevant. Electronic publication date.

- **Print-source article from a CD-ROM periodical database**

Selding, Peter B. de. "Arianespace Prepares for Changes in Market." *Space News* 8 Jan 1996: 1. *Space News 1994-96.* Record 7/1524. CD-ROM. Army Times. 1997.

General pattern for material from a periodical portable database (CD-ROM, diskette, magnetic tape) when no print source is indicated

Author(s). "Title of material accessed." Date if given. <u>Database title</u>. Publication medium (CD-ROM, diskette, or magnetic tape). Name of vendor if relevant. Electronic publication date.

- **Information from a CD-ROM periodical database, no print source evident**

"Goddard, Robert H." *Compton's Interactive Encyclopedia.* 1996 ed. CD-ROM. Compton's-Tribune. 1995.

General pattern for material from a nonperiodical portable database (CD-ROM, diskette, magnetic tape)

Author(s). Title of the part of the work, if relevant, underlined or in quotation marks. <u>Title of the product</u>. Edition, release, or version if relevant. Publication medium (CD-ROM, diskette, or magnetic tape). Place: publisher, year.

- **Information from a CD-ROM nonperiodical database**

"Dickinson, Emily." *The Concise Columbia Encyclopedia. Microsoft Bookshelf '95.* 1995 ed. CD-ROM. Redmond: Microsoft, 1995.

"Meat." *The Oxford English Dictionary.* 2nd ed. CD-ROM. Oxford: Oxford UP, 1992.

MacArthur, Douglas. "On Landing on Leyte." 17 Oct. 1944. *Bartlett's Familiar Quotations.* Boston: Little, 1992. Expanded multimedia ed. CD-ROM. New York: Time, 1995.

"Seattle Aquarium / Pier 59." *AAA Map 'n' Go.* Ver. 3.0. American Automobile Assn., 1997. CD-ROM. Yarmouth, ME: DeLorme, 1997.

Audiovisual Materials

Audiovisual medium names include CD (compact disk), audiocassette, audiotape (reel-to-reel tape), LP (long-playing record), videocassette, videodisk, filmstrip, sound filmstrip, film, and slide program. The *MLA Handbook* does not require a medium designation for compact disks or for films, but the information may be helpful.

If you are focusing on a particular person, cite that person first. If needed for clarification, add an abbreviation for the person's contribution, such as cond[uctor], dir[ector], narr[ator], perf[ormer], and prod[ucer]. Persons and performing groups can also be mentioned after the title of the work.

General pattern for audiovisual materials

Person of interest if applicable. <u>Title</u>. Other persons and groups as applicable. Medium. Producer or manufacturer, date.

- **Compact disk**

Morning Songbirds. Rec. Kim Wilson. CD. LaserLight-Delta, 1993. [Kim Wilson recorded the birds.]

- **Selection on a compact disk**

"Rain with Pygmy Owl." *Morning Songbirds.* Rec. Kim Wilson. CD. LaserLight-Delta, 1993.

- **Audiocassette**

Mozart, Wolfgang A. *The Early Symphonies.* Vol. 1, cassette 1. Cond. Neville Marriner. Academy of St. Martin-in-the-Fields. Rec. 1972-73. Audiocassette. Musical Heritage Society, 1990.

- **Selection on an audiocassette**

Mozart, Wolfgang A. Symphony no. 1 in E-flat major, K. 16. *The Early Symphonies.* Vol. 1, cassette 1. Cond. Neville Marriner. Academy of St. Martin-in-the-Fields. Rec. 1972-73. Audiocassette. Musical Heritage Society, 1990. [A song selection would be in quotation marks, and a named symphony (e.g., Mozart's *Prague* Symphony) would be underlined and capitalized like a book title. The symphony in this example has no underlining since it is not identified by a specific name.]

- **Videocassette**

Public Trust or Private Property. Prod. On Television, Ltd.
    Videocassette. California Newsreel, 1988.

- **Videocassette series**

The Story of English. Narr. Robert MacNeil. 9 PBS programs. 5
    videocassettes. MacNeil-Lehrer/BBC, 1986.

Unpublished and Oral Communications

Letter, memo, or e-mail

Austerman, Charles E. Letter to the author. 14 Apr. 1998.
Eisenhower, Dwight David. Letter to Robert F. Collins. 8 Feb. 1958.
Delaney, Morris. "Adverbs Again." E-mail to the author. 13 May 1996.

Interview that you conducted

Helms, Jesse. Telephone interview. 29 July 1997.
Updike, Theresa S. Personal interview. 3 Feb. 1998.

Public address

Hallas, Ramona. "Teaching English as a Second Language." Indiana
    Assn. of Christian Schools Convention. Colonial Christian
    School, Indianapolis. 25 Sept. 1997.
Dougherty, David F. "Willingly Ignorant of Creation and the Flood."
    Sermon. Faith Baptist Church, Minneapolis. 22 Feb. 1998.

CHAPTER 3

Science Writing

Because *doing* science requires care—exact procedures, accurate measurement, and so on—it is often assumed that research writing about science must be more difficult and more technical than other kinds of research writing. However, although science writing has certain specific requirements, it is essentially like other kinds of academic writing. This chapter points out an important general principle and then discusses some specifics about science writing.

Clarity

As in other academic areas, the most important characteristic of good science writing is clarity. Clarity comes mainly from being simple and direct, trying to say complicated things clearly. It comes, we might say, from placing clear words in clear sentences. Listen to an editor and publisher of scientific books and journals:

> The beauty of science is in the science, not in the language used to describe it. The beauty of English is its ability, when properly used, to express the most complicated concepts in relatively clear words and to point up the beauty of the science.[1]

In addition to clear individual sentences, another aid to clarity is logical organization, especially when supported by smooth, clear transitions.

> You can achieve clear communication, which is the prime objective of scientific reporting, by presenting ideas in an orderly manner and by expressing yourself smoothly and precisely. By developing ideas clearly and logically and leading readers smoothly from thought to thought, you make the task of reading an agreeable one.[2]

In the next section we will explain how to organize a paper that reports on experimentation.

The style guide of the American Chemical Society mentions several principles to aid in clear, effective writing: Use words in their usual meanings, and do not use slang or jargon. Vary your sentence length, but avoid long sprawling sentences. Be concise, using strong verbs and avoiding the passive voice when you can. Omit personal opinions and unnecessary phrases like "I believe" and "we concluded," but use the first person if it aids clarity: "Jones reported xyz, but I/we found. . . ." Finally, use tenses consistently.[3]

The importance of clarity in scientific writing cannot be over-emphasized. "Successful scientific experimentation is the result of a clear mind attacking a clearly stated problem and producing clearly stated conclusions."[4]

Organization of a Scientific Paper

For several decades there has been a standard organization for nearly all scientific papers in research journals. This organization is standard also for most student papers about original experiments, including a written report for a science project. After the title and the abstract (a brief summary of the paper), the heart of the paper can be summarized by the acronym *IMRaD* (IM-rad).

The IMRaD format includes Introduction, Materials and Methods, Results, and Discussion. This organization helps readers know what to expect, and it fits the experimental method well. The Introduction tells what problem or question was studied. The Materials and Methods section tells how it was studied. The Results section gives the findings from the study, and the Discussion tells what the findings mean. (The word *Abstract* and the four IMRaD section names should appear as section headings in your paper, either at the left margin or centered.)

The paper's **Title** should be brief but informative. Include the plant, animal, or material you studied, how you treated it, and what you measured. Leave out unnecessary phrases like "A Study of," "Effect of," and "Different Kinds of." For example, instead of "Measurement of Mouse Growth in Relation to Different Amounts of Dietary Vitamin C," the title could be "Vitamin C and Mouse Growth."

The **Abstract** briefly summarizes your project in one paragraph of 150 words or less. It should be written after the rest of the paper is done. It provides a very brief summary of the four IMRaD sections of your paper. That is, it tells the main purpose and scope of the project, describes the methods you used, summarizes the results, and states the main conclusions.

The **Introduction** provides some basic information about the subject and clearly states the purpose of the experiment. As you describe the problem you investigated, try to give some sense of why it is important. You may also state what your hypothesis was (your educated guess of what the results would be).

The **Materials and Methods** section states the materials you used and the procedures you followed in the experiment. You can be fairly brief, but you should give enough information for someone else to be able to repeat your experiment and get the same results.

The **Results** section briefly tells the outcome of your experiment. You should focus on the facts that are most meaningful. Remember the advantages of graphs, tables, and illustrations, which can make it easy for your reader to see what happened.

In the **Discussion** section you tell the significance of what happened. Why did you get those results, and what did you learn from them? You can also discuss whether the results agreed with your hypothesis.

At the end come the **References,** listing all the articles and books that gave you information you used in the experiment. Your teacher will probably tell you which reference style to use; if not, you can choose one. In either case, follow the form carefully.

Tenses

Tenses are important in scientific papers. The basic principle is that you **report your work in the past tense,** but you **use the present tense for conclusions from previously published work** (established facts). The reason is that a scientific paper previously published in a primary journal is presumed to be established as knowledge (unless of course it was later disproved). Established knowledge is given the courtesy of the present tense, similar to the present tense for timeless truths ("The sun *sets* in the west.") Therefore, you would say, "Jackson showed that two-week-old bean plants *die* when deprived of water for one week."

Your own work, which has not (yet) been published in a primary journal, is reported in the past tense. That is, you use the past tense to state your procedures and your results: "The ten pots *were* turned on their sides in a uniform-light environment. After twenty-four hours all ten bean plants *were* curved upward." However, verbs that refer to tables and other displays are in the present tense ("Table 2 *shows* that the male mice *were* more aggressive than the females")—although a more concise sentence avoids that verb entirely: "Male mice were more aggressive than females (Table 2)."

Because of these principles, you will use both past and present tenses. The Abstract will refer to your results in the past tense. Similarly, the Materials and Methods and the Results sections will be mainly in the past tense, telling what you did and what you found. However, the

Introduction and the Discussion will use mainly the present tense because they normally focus on knowledge that is already established.

The Science Fair Poster

Besides the written project report, for a science fair you will also need to prepare a poster or self-standing display board. The poster or display board will have most of the same parts as the project report, but some sections will be shorter.

If you can, print out the sections as well as the tables and graphs on a computer printer for a good appearance; otherwise, type the poster sections and neatly draw the tables and graphs. Trim the page for each section so that you have about a one-inch margin on all four sides. For legibility, use black type on white paper, and add color by using colored poster board as the background. Either use a computer to print a title in large type or use press-down letters. You might also make your section headings somewhat larger or bolder.

You can do the Abstract and the Introduction separately or together on one page with individual headings. The Materials and Methods section should be separate, but you can give less detail than in the report if you display your equipment at the science fair. To save space, you might want to integrate the last two parts into one Results and Discussion section. Also, because of the limited poster space, references usually appear only in the written report.

The Background Research Paper

Sometimes a background research paper is a required part of a science project. This is similar in purpose to the "review of the literature" in the Introduction section of a scientific paper written by an established scientist.

The purpose of the background research paper is to help you gather as much information as possible on your topic before you do your own experimentation. Knowing the existing research, theories, and discoveries will help you focus your investigation on an interesting area that has not already been fully explored. When you later write your science project report using IMRaD organization (see page 36), you will already have an excellent background for briefly giving some basic information about the subject in the Introduction section.

As a science researcher and writer, you will follow the same process as researchers in other areas of knowledge. That is, you will choose and narrow your topic, find good sources, take notes, organize your notes and your paper in whatever way works best, write the paper and the source references, and revise and polish the paper. The flow chart and discussion in Chapter 1, "Research Writing: The Whole Process," will take you through the process step by step.

In looking for information about your science topic, begin with your textbooks and encyclopedias, looking for general information and ideas for other sources. Then go to your school library, the public library, and (if possible) a nearby university library. Look for both books and periodicals. Keep in mind that news magazines, *Reader's Digest,* and health magazines often include clear discussions of timely scientific subjects.

As you look for science information sources, remember the U.S. government. Many departments and agencies publish extensively, including the Departments of Agriculture, Commerce (including yearly earthquake information), Defense, Education, Health and Human Services, the Interior, State, and the Treasury (alcohol and tobacco information). Other government sources for scientific documents include the Atomic Energy Commission, Fish and Wildlife Service, Bureau of Mines, National Aeronautic and Space Administration, National Oceanographic and Atmospheric Administration (weather information), Public Health Service, and the military services.

Among the indexes of government material are the *Cumulative Subject Index, Index to U.S. Government Periodicals, Monthly Catalog,* and *Publications Reference File.* If you find a reference and the library has the book or pamphlet you need, you may be able to check it out; but if not, you may photocopy it since publications of the government are not copyrighted. Also, many government publications are available for purchase, but be sure to allow plenty of time (several weeks) to receive the material you order.

Other sources of scientific information are professional organizations, specialized charitable organizations, and certain corporations; these often have free pamphlets available. When you find a good source, enclose a large SASE (self-addressed stamped envelope) with your letter of request.

Since this research paper is part of your science project, your teacher will probably want you to mention the experiment you plan to do. If so, here is how to work it in. The introduction paragraph to your background research paper should be like a funnel: beginning broadly with the general subject, and progressively narrowing down to your specific topic. In the paragraph after that, briefly tell about your planned experiment. Then follow your outline, paragraph by paragraph, logically presenting the background information for the experiment. The final paragraph or two should summarize your facts and predict what your experiment will prove or disprove.

Documentation Styles

Research writers in every field—such as science or history or English—need to indicate what sources they have used. The citations in the text (the body of the paper) should be clear but not interrupt unnecessarily. The list of references must give all the essential information clearly and efficiently. There is nearly infinite variety in documentation styles in the scholarly journals, but those who are not specialists (graduate students and professional researchers) can pick a standard style and follow it consistently.

Those who do science writing for classes or for science fairs need to find out from their teachers which documentation style is required. Your teacher will probably choose one of the standard documentation styles (such as MLA or CBE) and require you to follow it.

Chapter 4, "Documenting Sources in the Sciences," gives specific information about how to cite sources in the text and then how to describe them in the reference list.

Chapter Three Notes

[1] Robert A. Day, *Scientific English: A Guide for Scientists and Other Professionals,* 2d ed. (Phoenix: Oryx, 1995) x.

[2] *Publication Manual of the American Psychological Association,* 4th ed. (Washington: American Psychological Assn., 1994) 23.

[3] Janet S. Dodd, ed., *The ACS Style Guide: A Manual for Authors and Editors* (Washington: American Chemical Soc., 1986) 2-3.

[4] Robert A. Day, *How to Write and Publish a Scientific Paper,* 4th ed. (Phoenix: Oryx, 1994) 1.

CHAPTER 4

Documenting Sources in the Sciences

Citations in the Text

In the sciences, references may be cited in the body of the paper in one of three different ways:

By parenthetical number:

> Then the complete process was fully described (3).

By superscript number:

> Then the complete process was fully described.[3]

By parenthetical author name and publication date:

> Then the complete process was fully described (Jenkins and Rich 1992).

Individual journals—even within the same field, such as chemistry—set their own requirements. A science teacher therefore may specify any one of these (or he may ask his students to use another style, such as MLA).

The most common ordering system for numerical citations, **citation order,** begins with number 1 and assigns numbers to new sources consecutively throughout the paper. A second or third reference to the same source reuses the number originally assigned to that source. (The other ordering system is alphabetical: numbers are assigned to the sources in alphabetical order and then used in the text where needed.)

Unless your science teacher gives you different instructions, we suggest that you use parenthetical numbers (the first example above) in citation order. You may still mention the author or the date in your sentence when desired.

> Jenkins and Rich (3) first described the complete process.
>
> The complete process was first described in 1992 (3).

As illustrated here, the source number should appear in the sentence wherever it is most relevant.

To cite more than one source, place the numbers in numerical order. A space follows a comma in parenthetical number citations but not in superscript number citations.

> Several investigators (3-5, 9) noted problems with the established method of measurement.

> Several investigators[3-5,9] noted problems with the established method of measurement.

Multiple name-and-date citations are given in chronological order.

> Several investigators (Brown 1987; Taber and Wesson 1988a; Tarkley and others 1998) noted problems with the established method of measurement.

In the citation just above, *1988a* refers to the first cited publication of Taber and Wesson in 1988; in the paper's reference list the date for that source again appears as *1988a*. (The next listed 1988 source by Taber and Wesson is dated *1988b*.) This way of marking dates is needed only in papers using name-and-date citations.

The Reference List

The reference list at the end of a science paper is usually called References or References Cited. Numbered sources appear in numerical order. If the citation numbers in the text are parenthetical, the reference numbers are followed by periods without parentheses. If citation numbers in the text are superscript, the numbers in the reference list can be either superscript or on the line with periods.

If name-and-date citations are used, the references are listed alphabetically by the last name of the first author. Sources by the same author—or exactly the same group of authors—are listed in chronological order. These alphabetical entries have underhung indentation as in MLA style.

The form for entries in the reference list varies from one journal to another. Because of this situation, books and booklets on science writing for students tend to do the following: (1) tell students to follow their teacher's instructions; (2) mention a few style manuals in the sciences; and (3) make up their own forms for the reference list, usually forms not very different from MLA style. This book provides a sample of three actual science styles and then extended information on one of them.

Your teacher will probably specify which style you should follow for citations and references (MLA, CBE, or some other). Even if you are allowed to choose, you will need to follow your chosen style very carefully. Following a style with care ensures that you include all needed information. Following it consistently keeps your readers from being confused by your notation. Care and consistency also show your professionalism.

When you type up the reference list at the end of your paper, begin on a new page. Type the centered heading *References* or *References Cited* one inch from the top of the page. Double-space down to the first entry. As in the rest of the paper, everything in the reference list is double-spaced. The entry number is at the left margin (one inch from the edge of the paper); if it is the usual full-sized numeral on the line, it is followed by a period. The entry itself begins five pica or six elite spaces from the left margin, and any following lines come to the same indented position. Examples in the next section illustrate that indention.

Three Samples

For easy comparison, references to the same book and the same journal article appear in the three sampled styles. The article is from the *Journal of Motor Behavior,* volume 29 (for 1997), issue number 1 (for March), pages 5-16. Because the whole volume is paged continuously (instead of starting at 1 in each issue), the month and the issue number are not needed.

Journal titles of more than one word are abbreviated in science references. A number of standard abbreviations are used, such as *J* for *Journal, Chem* for *Chemistry, Biochem* for *Biochemistry,* and *Phy* for *Physics.* Articles, conjunctions, and unimportant prepositions are dropped. Thus the *Journal of Motor Behavior* is given as *J Motor Behav* or *J Mot Behav.* Some journals require periods with abbreviations, and others use no periods.

The following sample styles are from three different fields: the life sciences (CBE style), chemistry (ACS style), and physics (AIP style).

CBE style

CBE style is based on *Scientific Style and Format: The CBE Manual for Authors, Editors, and Publishers,* 6th ed. (New York: Cambridge UP, 1994), produced by the Council of Biology Editors. The sixth edition of the CBE manual states that it covers the physical sciences and mathematics as well as the life sciences. However, it gives primary coverage to "the plant sciences, zoology, microbiology, and the medical sciences" (CBE 3). CBE recommendations influence the varied journal styles in the life sciences and medicine.

- **Books**

  1. Sutton A, Sutton M. Eastern forests. New York: Knopf; 1985. 638 p.

- **Periodicals**

  2. Berg WP, Alessio HM, Mills EM, Tong C. Correlates of recurrent falling in independent community-dwelling older adults. J Motor Behav 1997;29:5-16.

Because CBE style is designed to save space, it has less punctuation for authors and fewer spaces in the facts of journal publication. Only the first word of an article title or a book title is capitalized. In the first entry above, *638 p.* tells how many pages are in the whole book.

The CBE manual specifies the elements above, including ordering and punctuation, and "do[es] not specify type styles" (CBE 632). The manual acknowledges that some journals require italic type (or underlining) for titles of books and journals. CBE style is developed more fully, with two minor modifications, in the next section.

ACS style

ACS style comes from *The ACS Style Guide: A Manual for Authors and Editors* (Washington, DC: American Chemical Society, 1986), edited by Janet S. Dodd for the American Chemical Society. It influences the varied styles found in the field of chemistry.

- **Books**

  1. Sutton, A.; Sutton, M. Eastern Forests. New York: Knopf, 1985; pp 410-417.

- **Periodicals**

  2. Berg, W.P.; Alessio, H.M.; Mills, E.M.; Tong, C. J Motor Behav 1997, 29, 5-16.

Article titles are omitted in ACS style. Much more punctuation is used for authors' names than in CBE style. No period follows *p* (for page) or *pp* (for pages), used in referring to the relevant section(s) of the book.

AIP style

AIP style derives from the *AIP Style Manual,* 4th ed. (New York: American Institute of Physics, 1990). It influences the varied styles found in the field of physics.

- **Books**

    [1] A. Sutton and M. Sutton, <u>Eastern Forests</u> (Bantam, New York, 1985), pp. 410-417.

- **Periodicals**

    [2] W. P. Berg, H. M. Alessio, E. M. Mills, and C. Tong, J Motor Behav 29, 5-16 (1997).

Like ACS style, AIP style omits article titles. It also uses normal order for authors' first and last names. The date comes at or near the end, as shown.

Further Source Information

Scientific Style and Format: The CBE Manual is available from Cambridge University Press through most bookstores or from 40 West Twentieth Street, New York, New York 10011-4211. *The ACS Style Guide* is available from ACS, 1155 Sixteenth Street, NW, Washington, District of Columbia 20036. The *AIP Style Manual* is available from AIP, 335 East Forty-fifth Street, New York, New York 10017.

Mathematicians may be interested in *A Manual for Authors of Mathematical Papers* (Providence, RI: American Mathematical Society, 1990), available from AMS, Post Office Box 1571, Annex Station, Providence, Rhode Island 02901.

A Recommended Reference Style for Science Writing

Because of the thoroughness and wide use of the CBE manual, and because of the CBE style's conciseness and practicality, we explain this style in some detail. As noted above, CBE style is from *Scientific Style and Format: The CBE Manual for Authors, Editors, and Publishers,* 6th ed. (1994), by the Council of Biology Editors.

The following discussion has two minor differences from CBE specifications. First, although the CBE manual does not specify type styles, we recommend using standard italics or underlining for titles of books, journals, and other independent publications. Second, when only part of a book is relevant, we recommend stating the page numbers of the useful section, rather than the total number of pages in the book.

Underlining is the typed equivalent of italic print. If your computer or typewriter is able to produce italics, use them. This book uses underlining in the general patterns and italics in the specific examples.

In CBE style duplicate digits are not repeated in inclusive pages. That is, use *146-9* for *146-149*, and *1297-302* for *1297-1302*.

Books

The forms here apply also to booklets and pamphlets.

General pattern for a book

Author(s) [or editor(s)]. Title. Place of publication: publisher name; year. Pages used. [if you use part of the book]

Author(s) [or editor(s)]. Title. Place of publication: publisher name; year. Total pages. [if you use or refer to the whole book]

However, if you use name-and-date citation in the text, the year is placed after the author(s). If your teacher wants you to use this variation, you will need to apply it to all of your listed references. Here is the general book pattern, with an example:

Author(s) [or editor(s)]. Year. Title. Place of publication: publisher name. Pages used.

Galkin YA, Jennings VM. 1993. *Electrochemistry today.* New York: Pergamon. p 349-57.

• Books with authors

Galkin YA, Jennings VM. *Electrochemistry today.* New York: Pergamon; 1993. p 349-57. [pages 349-57 used]

Hargis W. *Major diseases of fish in Chesapeake Bay.* Baltimore: Williams & Wilkins; 1985. 159 p. [159 pages in book; whole book relevant]

• Books with editors

Harter VD, Rupp DT, Matthews JK, editors. *Oceanic temperature variations.* Chicago: Open Court; 1998. p 113-21, 311-2.

• Book with author, editor, translator, and note

Guili J. *Fish of the Mainit River.* Collins GC, translator; Marcos PD, editor. Washington: Worldwide; 1979. 146 p. Translation of: *Isda' na Mainit.*

- ### Edition; city of publication clarified

  Esterhazy TR. *Solar energy for all.* 2nd ed. Emmaus (PA): Rodale; 1979. p 193-209.

- ### Organization as author; parenthesized series and volume

  International Organization for Standardization. *Statistical methods.* Geneva: International Standards Organization; 1979. (ISO standards handbooks: 3).

- ### Microform

  Voegtlin DF. *Classification of antibiotics* [microfilm]. Elmsford (NY): Microforms International; 1995. 1 reel: 16 mm.

- ### Volume in a series

  Williams A. *Rice in southeast Asia.* Volume 3, *Improved crop varieties in the developing world.* New York: J Wiley; 1984. [pages used can appear here]

- ### Chapter or other part with separate title, same author(s)

  Johnson GW, Marshall PR. *Color spectroscopy.* 3rd ed. New York: Pergamon; 1991. Part B, Prismatic effects; p 33-45. [semicolon before the pages because the pages refer to the immediately preceding section title]

- ### Chapter or other part with different author(s)

  Fawzi A. The development of zero. In: Richards MW, Pachter FE, editors. *History of mathematical concepts.* 2nd ed. New York: Viking; 1969. p 15-27.

Scholarly Journals

In reference lists of scientific articles, journal titles of more than one word are abbreviated by using standard abbreviations and dropping articles, conjunctions, and unimportant prepositions. Unless your teacher tells you otherwise, you should abbreviate the titles of scholarly journals (but not nonscholarly magazines and newspapers).

In addition to *J, Chem,* and *Phy* (Journal, Chemistry, Physics), some other standard abbreviations are *Agric* (Agriculture, Agricultural), *Am* (American), *Assoc* (Association), *Bot* (Botanical, Botany), *Bull* (Bulletin), *Can* (Canadian), *Environ* (Environment[al]), *Inorg* (Inorganic), *Int* (International), *Lab* (Laboratory), *Nat* (National, Natural), *Org* (Organic), *Organ* (Organization), *Res* (Research), *Rev*

(Review), *Sci* (Science, Scientific), *Soc* (Social, Society), *Stud* (Studies), and *Univ* (University).

Drop *-ogy* to get the abbreviation for disciplines such as biology, entomology, geology, meteorology, pharmacology, physiology, and zoology; and use the same abbreviation for their adjectives ending in *-ogical.* Abbreviate other words by dropping at least the last two letters, leaving enough of the word for clarity. If you are unsure how to abbreviate, you can spell the word out.

Use only the first three letters of a month name.

General pattern for a journal article

Author(s). Article title. <u>Journal title</u> year month-if-needed day-if-any;volume number(issue number if needed):inclusive pages. [Month and issue are stated only if journal is paged by issue.]

However, if you use name-and-date citation in the text, the year is placed after the author(s). If your teacher wants you to use this variation, you will need to apply it to all of your listed references. Here is the general pattern for journal articles, with an example:

Author(s). Year. Article title. <u>Journal title</u> volume number(issue number if paged by issue):inclusive pages.

Lytle LA, Eldridge AL, Kotz K, Piper J, Williams S, Kalina B. 1997. Children's interpretation of nutrition messages. *J Nutr Educ* 29:128-36.

• Journal article

Lytle LA, Eldridge AL, Kotz K, Piper J, Williams S, Kalina B. Children's interpretation of nutrition messages. *J Nutr Educ* 1997;29:128-36.

• Organization as author

American Association of Colleges of Nursing. Indicators of quality in doctoral programs in nursing. *J Professional Nurs* 1997;13:200-2.

• Anonymous author

[Anonymous]. Manuscript preparation guidelines. *J Radio Stud* 1997;4:310-1.

• Article in a journal paged by issue

Diels J, Bernstein R, Stahlkopf KE, Zhao XM. Lightning control with lasers. *Sci Am* 1997 Aug;227(2):50-5.

Other Periodicals

General patterns for newspaper and magazine articles

Author(s). Article title. <u>Newspaper title</u> date of publication;section:page number(column number).

Author(s). Article title. <u>Magazine title</u> date of publication:page numbers.

• Signed newspaper article

Neergaard L. Discarded drug protein may protect diabetics. *Greenville News* (SC) 1997 July 25;Sect A:1(col 1).

• Unsigned newspaper article

[Anonymous]. New drug helps in treating arthritis. *Indianapolis Star* 1997 July 17;Sect A:7(col 2-4).

• Magazine article

Horvitz LA. Are animal advocates biting the hand of dedicated docs? *Insight on the News* 1997 May 19;13(18):40-1. [*or:* 1997 May 19:40-1.]

Electronic Publications

This section includes basic patterns from the CBE manual, updated slightly in line with current technology and practices.

Trademarked or copyrighted titles that are fully capitalized on-screen or on the title page of the documentation are fully capitalized in references. Availability information for online sources can be the protocol and address with access path (as in the following examples) or the name and city of the information service.

General patterns for electronic-journal articles and electronic books

Author(s). Article title. <u>Abbreviated journal title</u> [type of medium] date of publication;volume number(issue number):inclusive pages or other locator such as document number. Availability statement. Date accessed.

Author(s) if any. <u>Book title</u> [type of medium]. Place: publisher; year [when updated if applicable]. Section consulted if applicable. Availability statement. Date accessed.

• Electronic-journal article

Ray T, Huntley AC. WWW resources for dermatology: a critical appraisal. *Dermatol Online J* [serial online] 1995 Jul;1(1):Doc nr 3. http://matrix.ucdavis.edu/DOJvol1num1/internet-appraisal.html. Accessed 1997 Aug 5.

- **Electronic book**

    THE MERCK MANUAL OF DIAGNOSIS AND THERAPY [monograph online]. 16th ed. Whitehouse Station (NJ): Merck; 1992. Internet version. Merck; 1997. http://www.merck.com/pubs/mmanual/. Accessed 1997 Aug 5.

- **Part of electronic book**

    THE MERCK MANUAL OF DIAGNOSIS AND THERAPY [monograph online]. 16th ed. Whitehouse Station (NJ): Merck; 1992. Internet version. Merck; 1997. Hemorrhagic disorders; monograph nr 96 [2 paragraphs]. http://www.merck.com/pubs/mmanual/. Accessed 1997 Aug 5.

General pattern for computer programs

    Author(s) if any. Title [type of medium]. Edition or version. Place of publication: publisher; date of publication. Physical description. Accompanying material. Notes.

- **Computer program**

    Kiplinger TaxCut [computer program]. Filing edition tax year 1996; Windows version 1.1. Boston: Block Financial; 1997. 4 computer disks: 3.5 in. Accompanied by: 1 quick start guide; 1 1996 electronic filing procedures. System requirements: 386SX PC or faster; Windows 3.1, Windows 95, or Windows for work groups; 4MB RAM (8MB recommended); VGA monitor or better; 15MB available disk space; a mouse. Supports Windows-compatible printers; prints IRS-acceptable forms on plain paper.

Audiovisual Materials

The pattern for audiovisual materials is different in that the title is always first, before any authors or editors. The CBE manual gives these sample types of medium: audiocassette, filmstrip, motion picture, videocassette, videodisk, and videotape. The physical description can include the number of cassettes or reels, followed (after a colon and a space) by the running time, sound or color information, tape width, speed, and other relevant information.

General pattern

    Title [type of medium]. Author(s) and/or editor(s). Producer (if corporate and different from publisher). Place: publisher; date. Physical description. (Series statement if available). Accompanying material. Availability statement if applicable.

- **Compact disk**

  Morning songbirds [compact disk]. Wilson K, recorder. Santa Monica (CA): LaserLight-Delta Music, 1993. 1 compact disk: 46 min, digitally recorded bird songs. (Echoes of nature; CD 12150). Available from: Delta Music Inc., Santa Monica, CA 90404-3061.

- **Videocassette**

  Public trust or private property [videocassette]. On Television, producer. San Francisco: California Newsreel; 1988. 56 min. Available from: California Newsreel, 149 Ninth Street/420, San Francisco, CA 94103.

INDEX